The French Neutrals

IN

PENNSYLVANIA.

IN the notes to the edition of Mr. Longfellow's poem of Evangeline, published in London in 1853, I find the following statement. Speaking of the Acadian exiles, the annotator says:

"One thousand arrived in Massachusetts Bay, and became a public expense, owing, in a great degree, to an unchangeable antipathy to their situation, which prompted them to reject the usual beneficiary but humiliating establishment of paupers for their children. They landed in a most deplorable condition at Philadelphia. The government of the colony, to relieve itself of the charge such a company of miserable wretches would require to maintain them, proposed to sell them with their own consent; but when this expedient for their support was offered for their consideration, the neutrals refused it with indignation, alleging that they were prisoners, and expected to be maintained as such, and not forced to labour."

No Pennsylvanian can read this remarkable statement of what is assumed to be an historical fact, without a blush deeper than any other imputed misdeed excites, and as certainly will Pennsylvanians feel some solicitude to know if it be true or not. To show that it is utterly without foundation, is the object of this little essay; in which only incidentally do I mean to speak of that familiar tale of sorrow — the exile of the Acadian Neutrals in 1755. On reading the note which I have quoted, my first desire was to know how far Mr. Longfellow was responsible for it; and a Cambridge friend, of whom I made the inquiry, assured me that the poet disavowed all knowledge of it, the notes having first appeared in England. This was exactly what I expected; for among the tenderest and most beautiful passages in Evangeline (and to its exquisite beauty let me here bear my testimony) are those which describe the end of her pilgrimage, her lover's death within the sound of Christ Church bells, and the tomb of them both in the little Philadelphia churchyard. There is no trace in the poem of Pennsylvania's cruelty or her proffered sale to slavery.

I had to look elsewhere for the origin of the aspersion. In Judge Haliburton's History of Nova Scotia,[1] I at last found it in the very words used by the English annotator, and here — for no authority or document is cited — the responsibility must rest.

The best mode of refuting the accusation thus made against colonial Pennsylvania, is to tell, in a simple and perfectly authentic form, what did occur here, and in

[1] Haliburton's Nova Scotia, i. 183.

doing so to revive the memory — for every day, till Evangeline appeared, the tradition was becoming feebler — of as sad an episode as the modern world's great history affords. I know nothing more deeply pathetic; and we may wonder, with a sentiment kindred to religious awe, at the retribution on this deed of wrong, when, at the end of a century, we find Poetry stooping to pick up from oblivion the obscure tradition of the Acadian exiles, and writing it in characters of living light, to last forever.

Let any one look through accredited histories of the day, or even contemporary correspondence more recently published, and he will find no allusion to this Exodus of the Acadians. I have curiously examined, but in vain. Neither Lord Chesterfield, nor George Grenville, nor Horace Walpole, who says a good deal about American affairs in his light way, nor any letter-writer of the day, alludes to what was doing in the obscure corner of Nova Scotia. It was too humble a tragedy for the courtly gossipers of English society to trouble themselves about; and, so far as my studies go, there is no trace of it. The most that I find are a few allusions in the Gentleman's Magazine of 1756 and 1757. It occurred, let me note in passing, in a dismal and diminutive period of British story; and it is matter of pride to those who reverence (and what American student does not?) the grand, heroic character of the elder Pitt, that no part of this stain rests on his administration. It was far more characteristic of Newcastle and Bubb Doddington.

For my purposes I assume the reader to be familiar with the story of the French Neutrals down to the time when they left Acadia, and I therefore turn to Pennsylvania's welcome of them, whatever it was, merely premising that the number of exiles who left Nova Scotia early in September, 1755, was one thousand nine hundred and twenty-three—four hundred and eighty-three men, three hundred and thirty-seven women, and one thousand and fifty-three children. Of this number, one account says eight hundred came to Philadelphia; though my impression is, as I have said, that it was much less.

It was certainly an unpropitious time for French Roman Catholics to come to these Puritan or Protestant colonies. It was the day of natural as well as of unreasonable excitements. It was the time when an Indian and a Frenchman were looked on with equal horror. It was the day when the actual association did exist, and when within three hundred miles of Philadelphia and two from New York, French and Indians were advancing in victorious array. General Braddock was defeated in July, 1755, and every English settlement on the seaboard trembled for its existence. The English language and the Reformed Religion, for a time, seemed to be in danger all over the world, in America and in India. This was the actual state of things, and yet it may well be doubted whether even the hostile Frenchmen of those days had not worse designs attributed to them than they deserved. "May God," writes a gentleman in Philadelphia, after the panic had subsided, "be pleased to give us success against all our copper-coloured cannibals and French savages, equally cruel and perfidious in their natures."[1]

---

[1] Shippen Papers, 93.

Yet when, in 1756, Washington, then a provincial colonel, defeated a party of French and Indians and obtained possession of the French commander's instructions, they were found to contain these explicit words: "Le Sieur Donville employera tous ses Talents et tout son crédit à empêcher les Sauvages d'user d'aucun Cruauté, sur ceux qui tombéront entre leurs mains. L'Honneur et l'Humanité doivent en cela nous servir de guide;"[1] and again, later, in 1757, in the instructions found in the pocket of a French cadet, killed near Fort Cumberland: "Suppose qu'il fasse de Prisonniers il empêchera que les Sauvages de son Detachment n'exercent à leur Egard Aucune Cruauté Fait." One pauses pleasantly over these disinterred memorials of kind and merciful feeling so little looked for, softening the hideous front of savage warfare; but it must be recollected our terrified and excited ancestors knew nothing of them. What they knew, and were made to know, of Frenchmen and French Papists, is very clear from the exaggerated public documents and messages of the Colonial governors, who found no language strong enough wherewith to stir the sluggish liberality of the Assemblies, who raised money grudgingly, even when most frightened; or from pulpit oratory, never more acrimonious than then; or from such rumours as this, which I cut from a Philadelphia paper of September, 1755, a short time before the Roman Catholic exiles arrived, under date of Halifax.

"A few days since three Frenchmen were taken up and imprisoned on suspicion of having poisoned some wells in this neighbourhood. They are not tried yet, and it's

[1] Pennsylvania Archives, ii. 600.

imagined if they are convicted thereof, they will have but a few hours to live after they are once condemned." And the first rumour of the intention forcibly to remove the Acadians from their country, was accompanied with the statement that, from among them, "three Priests or Jesuits had been taken and sent to Halifax, and put on board the Admiral's ship for security."[1]

Admiral Boscawen's great armament of ships-of-the-line and frigates, was employed in awing unarmed peasants and capturing fugitive Jesuits! It was to an atmosphere of public feeling thus excited, that the poor exiles came. Let us see how they were heralded, how they arrived, how they were treated here in Philadelphia.

The first intimation, in a popular form, of the intention to drive the Acadians from their homes, is in a letter from Halifax, dated August 9th, and printed in the Pennsylvania Gazette of the 4th of September, 1755, the day before the memorable 5th of September, Col. Winslow's "day of great fatigue and trouble," when the meeting was held in the church at Grand Pré, and the doom was told.[2] It is as follows, and is very characteristic:

"We are now upon a great and noble scheme of sending the neutral French out of the Province, who have always been secret enemies, and have encouraged our savages to cut our throats. If we can effect their expulsion, it will be one of the greatest things that ever did the English in America; for, by all accounts, that part of the country they possess is as good land as any in the world: in case, therefore, we could get some good English farmers in their

---

[1] Pennsylvania Gazette, Sept. 4, 1755. [2] Haliburton, i. 335, 338.

room, this Province would abound in all sorts of provisions."

Between this date and the arrival of the exiles, I find no precise reference to the subject, though but little intermission of the inflammatory appeals to national and sectarian antipathies. It may be that the public mind was not a little excited by what seemed to be supernatural warning — an earthquake, which, in the early part of November, 1755, went round the world, devastating European cities, and at least startling those in America. The shock of an earthquake, the advent of a ship-load of Roman Catholics, and the news, utterly groundless as it must have been, which I find in the newspapers of the very day the exiles came, that the Indians and *French* had attacked Lancaster, prepared for them a sorry welcome.

On the 19th and 20th of November, 1755, three sloops, the Hannah, the Three Friends, and the Swan, arrived in the Delaware, with the Neutrals on board. They had cleared from Halifax. One of them, say the newspapers of the day, came up to town, but was immediately ordered down again. How the authorities at first received them can only be gathered from the Executive records; nothing of the action of the Assembly having survived, or being accessible, but its meagre journal. The Governor was Robert Hunter Morris, of whom it may at least be said, that he had had his full share of those deplorable squabbles with the popular representatives, which William Penn left as a continuing legacy to his family and successors. Governor Morris's administration had had also to encounter the trial of actual war close at hand. The arrival of the

Neutrals seems to have thrown him into a state of terrible alarm; and on the day the first cargo of them arrived, he thus wrote to Governor Shirley, having previously laid the matter before the Council:

"I wrote your Excellency a few days ago by Mr. Benzill; who, I hope, will find you safe at New York, since which two vessels are arrived here with upward of three hundred neutral French from Nova Scotia, who Governor Lawrence has sent to remain in this Province, and I am at a very great loss to know what to do with them. The people here, as there is no military force of any kind, are very uneasy at the thought of having a number of enemy's scattered in the very bowels of the country, who may go off from time to time with intelligence, and joyn their countrymen now employed against us, or foment some intestine commotion in conjunction with the Irish and German Catholics, in this and the neighbouring province. I, therefore, must beg your particular instructions in what manner I may best dispose of these people, as I am desirous of doing any thing that may contribute to his majesty's service. I have, in the mean time, put a guard out of the recruiting partys now in town, on board of each vessel, and ordered these neutrals to be supplied with provisions, which must be at the expense of the crown, as I have no Provincial money in my hands; for this service I have prevailed on Capt. Morris, who is recruiting here for Col. Dunbar's Regiment, to postpone the sending off his recruits till I could here from you upon the head, which I hope to do by the return of the post."[1]

[1] Pa. Arch. ii. 506; Colonial Records vi. 712.

We have not Shirley's answer, but there is some correspondence accidentally extant which shows that Governor Morris found at least one response to his anxieties and alarms at the sudden incursions of the poor exiles. The Chief Magistrate of the neighbouring province of New Jersey was Jonathan Belcher, the father of him who, as Chief Justice of Nova Scotia, according to Mr. Bancroft, had by his stern opinion that they were "rebels," and "recusants," fixed the doom of the Acadians. Father and son seem to have had harsh sympathies. On the 22d of November, Morris writes to Belcher very much to the same effect as he had written to Shirley, and the day but one after (25th) Belcher replies:

"I am truly surprised how it could ever enter the thoughts of those who had the ordering of the French Neutrals, or rather Traitors and Rebels to the crown of Great Britain, to direct any of them into these Provinces, where we have already too great a number of foreigners for our own good and safety. I think they should have been transported directly to old France, and I entirely coincide with your honor that these people would readily join with the Irish Papists, &c., to the ruin and destruction of the King's Colonies, and should any attempt to land here, I should think, in duty to the King and to his good people under my care, to do all in my power to crush an attempt."[1]

It is well none of the exiles wandered as far as Elizabethtown. They would have been effectually "crushed out" there.

---

[1] Pa. Arch. ii. 513.

On the 24th November, Gov. Morris made the arrival of the Neutrals the subject of a special message to the Assembly, informing them he did not think it safe to permit them to land; that he had ordered guards to be placed on the vessels below the town, and that in consequence of an alarm of sickness amongst the crowded sufferers, some of them had been landed at Province Island.

It is pleasant now to turn from this record of Proprietary harshness — this intolerant sympathy of Deputy Executives, to the action of the representatives of the people and of the people themselves; and here my defence of Pennsylvania properly begins.

The student of our colonial history need not be reminded of the dismal continuity of disputes between the Assembly and the Governors on the questions of taxation and supplies. It is hard to deduce any political principle from our records, unless it be new confirmation of the truth that all absenteeism, and all imitation of feudalism, with its manors, and its quit-rents, and its privileged estates, are especially uncongenial to our Pennsylvania habits of thought and action. It is scarcely worth while now to inquire who were right and who were wrong, for it is all swept away as part of the rubbish of our story. The poor Deputy Governors, agents of the Proprietaries, had a hard time. Exactions from the metropolitan authorities — actual invasion and danger on the one hand, and on the other, annoying resistance, and cavilling, and murmurs on the part of those who alone could raise revenue to meet their demands and requisitions. The Neutrals arrived, however, at a propitious moment. There happened to be a lull in the storm of controversy. On the very day that Governor Morris sent to the Assembly his message about the Neutrals, he communicated the soothing news that the Proprietaries, on hearing of General Braddock's defeat, had sent an order on the Receiver General for £5000, to be applied for the common safety. The Assembly was for the time pacified. They voted a new Bill of Supplies, and resolved at the same moment to make provision for the sustenance and protection of the Neutrals.[1]

I am proud to say that, in their relations to those unfortunate fugitives, I find on the records of the popular representative body no trace of the malignant animosity and sectarian antipathy which actuated the Executive. Painfully impracticable as Penn's principles had shown themselves when applied to periods of war and invasion, and danger from the strong and armed hand without, yet when the homeless fugitive and stranger came and asked a place of refuge, the beautiful feature of the Quaker character, charity, in its highest sense, and charity, too, which knows no difference of creed, seemed more beautiful than ever. The great principle of liberty of conscience and toleration was put in practice towards these exiled "Papists," and it certainly is very hard, with this unquestioned record before us, that the Friends of Pennsylvania should be now-a-days charged with mercenary inhumanity.

But our meagre records show there was another influence in favor of the exile. There were hereditary national sympathies at work aside from all matters of technical religion, which gave the French exiles in Philadelphia a

---

[1] Votes, 519, 523.

welcome that they had no right to expect. Papists or not, they were French men, and women, and children — and there were in Quaker garb, living in Philadelphia, men of French descent, who, though Huguenots, and sprung from that glorious race of men, the European Protestants of the sixteenth century, still felt kindly to those who were Frenchmen like themselves. The Benezets, and Lefevres, and De Normandies, of Philadelphia, came from the same soil years ago, as did the Landrys, and Galerms, and Le Blancs, and Melançons, and Thibodeaus, and accordingly I find that while the Assembly paused in no unreasonable delay of counsel, this minute is made.

"Antony Benezet, attending without, was called in, and informed the House that he had, at the request of some of the members, visited the French Neutrals now on board sundry vessels in the river, near the city, and found that they were in great want of blankets, shirts, stockings, and other necessaries; and he then withdrew, (whereupon) Resolved, That this House will allow such reasonable expenses as the said Benezet may be put to in furnishing the Neutral French now in the Province." [1]

Antony Benezet, the Huguenot Quaker, was the first almoner to these poor fugitives, and it was with no reluctant gratitude that one of their number, in the first memorial to the Assembly, said: — "Blessed be God that it was our lot to be sent to Pennsylvania, where our wants have been relieved, and we have, in every respect, been treated with Christian benevolence and charity." [2]

Nothing, however, beyond the general trust in Mr.

---

[1] Votes, 524. [2] Ibid, 538.

Benezet and the other citizens connected with him, was done; for early in December, the Assembly adjourned till March, 1756. Before they reassembled, it appears from the public accounts that at least £1000 currency had been expended for the relief of the Neutrals.[1]

The Assembly was convoked specially by the Governor early in February, and on the 11th, their attention was called to the Neutrals by a petition from one of their number, Jean Baptiste Galerm, and a list of the names of the individuals and the families of the exiles given. The petition is preserved in a translated form, but the list is unfortunately lost. The petition contains a brief and temperate statement of the causes which led to the exile of the Acadians, a strong expression of gratitude for the kindness with which they had been received, and a protestation of their passive loyalty (and more than this no one had a right to expect) to the British crown. It contains no prayer for specific assistance. A bill for the relief, or, as it is rather ambiguously expressed in its title, for "dispersing" the inhabitants of Nova Scotia into the counties of Philadelphia, Bucks, Chester, and Lancaster, was immediately introduced, and on the 5th of March, 1756, became a law by the Executive approval.[2]

This law is now before me, and I can see nothing in it but considerate kindness. The exiles were to be divided, not dispersed, among the counties designated, in order "to give them an opportunity of exercising their own labour

[1] See also Morris' Letter, 1st Feby., 1756, to Gov. Dinwiddie, Pa. Arch. 562.

[2] Votes, 537, 545.

and industry, and they were to be supported at the public expense, and among the commissioners named to carry it into execution were not only those who, as Friends, had been active in this and every scheme of benevolence, but those whose French descent and sympathies may be inferred from their names. Antony Benezet was not one, but there were Jacob Duché, and Thomas Say, and Abraham de Normandie, and Samuel Lefevre. There is nothing like a disruption of families hinted at. It was to continue in force twelve months, and no longer.

What exactly was done, or attempted under this act, there is no means of knowing. Down to July of this year, when Governor Denny arrived, upwards of £1200 had been spent in their support, and this too, although there were difficulties created by the exiles themselves, who, though willing to be supported as objects of charity, evidently thought — for this is the fair construction of their recorded conduct — that by refusing to work, they would force a recognition of their rights as prisoners of war, and as such be entitled to be exchanged or sent back to France. One cannot blame them for this sort of contumacy, and yet it made the duty of kindness and protection not an easy one. Governor Morris, who seems to have been an especial victim of the Gallophobia of his time, took his farewell of his function by letters to Lord Loudoun, the new Governor-General, and to Sir Charles Hardy, filled with alarms as to French spies and Papal influence. If any one now-a-days, afflicted with a fear of Romanistic or Foreign influences, will look back to the terrors of a century ago, he may, if capable of any rational process, learn a salutary lesson. "By means," writes Governor Morris, on 5th July, 1756, "of the Roman Catholicks who are allowed in this and the neighbouring Province of Maryland, the free exercise of their Religion, and therein the other privileges of English Freemen, the French may be made acquainted with the steps taken against them; nor do I see how it is possible to detect them, as from the head of Chesapeak Bay the roads thro' this Province to Potomic are open and much travelled, especially by Germans, who have a large settlement at Frederick town in Maryland, a frontier place near Kittochtinny Hills; none are examined who pass that way." To which Sir Charles, the Governor of New York, promptly replies: "I am inclined to think the Treasonable correspondence must have been carried on by some Roman Catholicks, and I have heard you have an Ingenious Jesuit in Philadelphia."[1] Let me here pause and ask which, now-a-days, seems most preposterous — Frederick town, in Maryland, being a frontier town, or an American Governor being afraid of a Jesuit! And yet both were so, one hundred years ago.

On the 27th of August, and on the 2d of September, the Neutrals addressed, in person, earnest and pathetic memorials both to the Assembly and the Executive Council. A candid examination of these papers, written with great eloquence and precision, satisfies me that they were meant not merely to tell their tale of actual sorrow, but to use, as I have already hinted, their sufferings as an argument for restoration to liberty, or their return to Europe. The two ideas are always closely interwoven.

[1] Pa. Arch. ii. 690, 694.

"We humbly pray," they say to the Assembly, "that you would extend your goodness so far as to give us leave to depart from hence, or be pleased to send us to our nation, or anywhere to join our country-people; but if you cannot grant us these favours, we desire that provision may be made for our subsistence so long as we are detained here. If this, our humble request, should be refused, and our wives and children be suffered to perish before our eyes, how grievous will this be! — had we not better have died in our native land?" They admit they have refused cows, and gardens, and modes of industry, because, say they, "we will never consent to settle here." To the Governor they spoke the same language of supplication and remonstrance; though one may almost suspect satire in their affectionate loyalty, when they beg to be suffered to join their own nation "in the same manner which it has pleased his Majesty, King George (*whom may God preserve!*), to cause us to be transported here contrary to our will."[1] The remonstrance, be its object what it may have been, had no effect; for, while the Assembly paused, the Governor sternly repelled the supplicants, with the decision that they could not and should not be treated as prisoners of war, and hinted to the Assembly that it was expedient that the Neutrals should be more generally dispersed.[2]

On the meeting of the Assembly in October, 1756, there is a sad revelation on its records of the sufferings of these poor people — made, too, not by them, but by one of the kindest of the voluntary almsgivers. It is the petition of

---

[1] Cōl. Rec. vii. 239.

[2] Ibid. vii. 241.

William Griffitts, one of the Commissioners. Disease and death had been busy among the exiles. Many had died of the small-pox, and, but for the care that had been bestowed on them, many more would have perished miserably. The overseers of the rural townships refused to receive them. The prejudice against the foreigners prevented the employment of those who were willing to work; "and many of them," says this paper, "have had neither meat nor bread for many weeks together, and been necessitated to pilfer and steal for the support of life."[1]

The simple Acadian farmers, who, in their once happy and secluded homes, a short year ago,

> "Dwelt in the love of God and of man,"

had become, or were becoming, mendicant pilferers in the streets of Philadelphia! It is piteous to think of the contrast.

This appeal again moved the Assembly, and in as short a time as the dilatory forms of legislation of the times permitted, a new bill was enacted, entitled an Act for binding out and settling such of the Inhabitants of Nova Scotia as are under age, and for maintaining the aged, sick, and maimed at the charge of the Province.[2]

It was of this measure—the compulsory binding out, to learn trades, of the children of those who could not support them—that the exiles most loudly complained; and the most elaborate remonstrance that is to be found on our records, was induced by it. It is a document of impassioned, and, to my mind, rather artificial rhetoric,

[1] Votes, 645.

[2] Ibid. 677, 685.

of which, as before, the key-note was a prayer for deliverance; but, let it be observed, no one word, from first to last, of complaint of personal or harsh treatment. "From this Province," they say, "we have experienced nothing but good; for which ourselves, our wives, and our children, shall not cease to supplicate the Almighty that He will heap upon you all blessings, spiritual and temporal."[1]

Hard as is the lot of the poor and incapable parent to be deprived temporarily of his children — especially hard is it where there are differences of language and religion — it is idle to deny the right and the duty of the Legislature, when the necessity arises, to make such compulsory provision. I confess I am unable to see what less or what else the Assembly could have done; and so, in their perplexity, they seemed to think; for, after a vain attempt to confer further with the Governor and his Council, and to ascertain what they thought best to be done, the whole subject was dropped. The Act of January, 1757, with a short supplement remedying some matter of detail, was the last legislative act, with the exception of constant and liberal appropriations of money, amounting, in six years, from November, 1755, to 1761, to the not inconsiderable sum of upwards of £7000; to which neither the Crown nor the Proprietaries, as far as I can discover, contributed a farthing — the first having its hands full with a European war and schemes of conquest, and the latter watching their estates and devising schemes, to use Thomas Penn's phrase in a letter to Mr. Hamilton, of "getting the better of the Assemblies."[2]

---

[1] Votes, 685. [2] Hamilton MSS: Letter, 25 February, 1755.

On or about the 7th of March, Pennsylvania and its capital were honored by the presence of the new commander-in-chief, a Peer of the Realm, John, Earl of Loudoun. His was the first coronet that had ever shone on this distant and simple land. There was feasting and rejoicing when he came, and around him no doubt clustered the loyal worshippers of rank and authority; but all the while, so say the legislative records, the poor Neutrals were pining away in misery—not the less intense because, in some measure, self-inflicted. On the 3d of March, 1757, the authorities were instructed by the Assembly to act for their relief, "so as to prevent them (these are the words of the resolution) from perishing from want."[1]

Lord Loudoun remained but a few days in Philadelphia, but quite long enough to inflict, by the exercise of his high powers, a new pang and a new indignity on the poor Neutrals. He, or rather Secretary Peters for him, found it necessary to ascertain the exact number of Roman Catholics in the Province, so that this terrible danger might be guarded against; and in the Colonial Records I find the following modest letter from the priest, which one would think might have lulled to rest the anti-papal elements of the time:

"Honored Sir:—I send you the number of Roman Catholics in this town, and of those whom I visit in the country. Mr. Sneider is not in town to give an account of the Germans, but I have heard him often say, that the whole number of Roman Catholics, English, Irish, and

[1] Votes, 700, 715.

Germans, including men, women, and children, does not exceed two thousand.

"I remain, ROBERT HARDY."

The poor remnant of French Neutrals did not seem worth counting!

The Earl of Loudoun was a fit representative of the ministry of that day; for he was utterly incapable, and perversely tyrannical. He was considered "a man of judgment and ability" by the Duke of Newcastle.[1] He was superseded promptly and contemptuously by Mr. Pitt, on his accession to office a few months later, who sent to America manly men to do his work of beneficent energy. It was Lord Loudoun of whom Dr. Franklin has preserved the traditionary jest, that he was like St. George on the signs, always on horseback and never advancing. He distrusted and disregarded Washington. He fretted Franklin. He was just the man for a little persecution of these poor exiled Neutrals. He was in Philadelphia, as I have said, but a few days; but long enough for his work of small despotism.

In the Colonial Records of 1757,[2] is a Sheriff's warrant, issued by the Governor, at the request of Lord Loudoun, directing the apprehension of Charles Le Blanc and Jean Baptiste Galerme, now in Philadelphia city; Philip Melançon, at Frankford; Paul Bujauld, at Chester; and Jean Landy, at Darby, as suspicious and evil-minded persons, who have uttered menacing speeches against his Majesty and his liege subjects. They are to be arrested and committed to jail.

[1] Chatham Correspondence, i. 237.

[2] Col. Rec. vii. 446.

To this warrant the Sheriff made no return that has been preserved; but the following curious and characteristic letter from Lord Loudoun, for which I am indebted, within the last few days, to Mr. Bancroft, and which has never before been made public, explains the act of wrong. There is in it something much more like a delivery of these poor people to slavery than anything that Pennsylvania annals afford. The indignity of petitioning in French sounds strangely to us of a century later.

The letter, however, speaks for itself:

[EARL OF LOUDOUN TO WILLIAM PITT.]

Extract.

"25th *April*, 1757.

"SIR— * * * * When I was at Pensilvania I found that the French Neutrals there had been very mutinous, and had threatened to leave the women and children and go over to join the French in the back country; they sent me a Memorial in French setting forth their grievances. I returned it and said I could receive no Memorial from the King's subjects but in English, on which they had a general meeting at which they determined they would give no Memorial but in French, and as I am informed they come to this resolution from looking on themselves entirely as French subjects.

"Captain Cotterell, who is Secretary for the Province of Nova Scotia, and is in this Country for the recovery of his health, found among those Neutrals one who had been a Spie of Colonel Cornwallis and afterwards of Governor

Lawrence, who he tells me had behaved well both in giving accounts of what those people were doing and in bringing them intelligence of the situation and strength of the French forts and in particular of Beausejour; by this man I learnt that there were five principal leading men among them who stir up all the disturbance these people make in Pensilvania, and who persuade them to go and join the enemy and who prevent them from submitting to any regulation made in the country, and to allow their children to be put out to work.

"On finding this to be the case, I thought it necessary for me to prevent, as far as I possibly conld, such a junction to the enemy: on which I secured those five ringleaders and put them on board Captain Talkingham's ship, the Sutherland, in order to his carrying them to England, to be disposed of as his Majesty's servants shall think proper; but I must inform you that if they are turned loose they will directly return and continue to raise all the disturbance in their power, therefore it appears to me that the safest way of keeping them would be to employ them as sailors on board ships of war.

LOUDOUN.

"The Right Hon.
"WILLIAM PITT.
(Indorsed) "R. July 6th."

It is quite possible that the men thus exiled (and of their fate there is no trace) may have been the leaders, the speakers, the writers for the exiles; for after they went away, there appears no recorded remonstrance or petition from the others. They wasted away in uncomplaining misery,—pensioners on charity. They are rarely referred to in public documents.

On the 9th of February, 1761, a committee of inquiry on the subject was appointed by the Assembly, and on the 26th they reported as follows:

"We, the committee appointed to examine into the state of the French Neutrals, and to report our opinion of the best method of lessening their expense to this province, have, in pursuance of the said appointment, made inquiry, and thereupon do report—

"That the late extraordinary expenses charged by the overseers of the poor, have been occasioned by the general sickness which prevailed amongst them, in common with other inhabitants, during the last fall and part of the winter; this, added to the ordinary expense of supporting the indigent widows, orphans, aged and decrepid persons, has greatly enlarged the accounts of this year. They have likewise a number of children, who, by the late acts of Assembly, ought to have been bound out to service, but their parents have always opposed the execution of these laws, on account of their religion; many of these children, when in health, require no assistance from the public; but in time of sickness, from the poverty of their parents, become objects of charity, and must perish without it.

"Your Committee called together a number of their chief men, and acquainted them with the dissatisfaction of the House on finding the public expense so much increased by their opposition to those laws, which were framed with a compassionate regard to them, and tending immediately to their ease and benefit, and assured them that, unless they could propose a method more agreeable to themselves for lightening the public burden, their children would be taken from them, and placed in such families as could maintain them, and some effectual method taken to prevent the ill effects of idleness in their young people.

"They answered, with appearance of great concern, that they were very sorry to find themselves so expensive to the good people of this Province; reminded us of the late general sickness as the principal cause of it, which they hoped might not happen again during their continuance here; that in expectation of lessening this expense, and of obtaining some restitution for the loss of their estates, they had petitioned the Court of Great Britain, and humbly remonstrated to his Majesty the state of their peculiar sufferings, and as the Governor had been so kind as to transmit and recommend their said petition and remonstrance, they doubted not but the King would be so gracious as to grant a part of their country, sufficient for their families to resettle on, where they flatter themselves they shall enjoy more health, and be free from the apprehensions of their children being educated in families whose religious sentiments are so different from theirs. In the mean time they pray the indulgence of the government in suffering them to retain their children, as they find, by experience, that those few who are in Protestant families, soon become estranged and alienated from their parents; and, though anxious to return to Nova Scotia, they beg to be sent to old France, or anywhere, rather than part with their children; and they promise to excite and encourage all their young people, to be industrious in acquiring a competency for their own and their parents' subsistence, that they may not give occasion for complaints hereafter. How far they may succeed in this, or their application to the Crown, is very uncertain. We are of opinion that nothing short of putting in execution the law, which directs the Overseers of the Poor to bind out their children, will so effectually lessen this expense, unless the Governor, with the concurrence of the Commander-in-Chief of the King's forces, shall think fit to comply with their request and transport them out of this Province.

"Nevertheless, your Committee being moved with compassion for these unhappy people, do recommend them to the consideration of the House, as we hope that no great inconvenience can arise from the continuance of the public charity towards them for a few months longer; and think it just to observe, that there are amongst them numbers of industrious labouring men, who have been, during the late scarcity of labourers, of great service in the neighbourhood of this city.

"Submitted to the House."[1]

I find but one other minute, and that tells a sad tale. I quote it in the simple words in which it appears on the Journal of Assembly. It is on the 4th of January, 1766:

"A petition from John Hill, of the city of Philadelphia, joiner, was presented to the House and read, setting forth that the petitioner has been employed from time to time

[1] Votes, 143.

to make coffins for the French Neutrals who have died in and about this city, and has had his accounts regularly allowed and paid by the Government, till lately; that he is now informed by the gentlemen commissioners, who used to pay him, that they have no public money in their hands for the payment of such debts; that he has made sixteen coffins since his last settlement (as will appear from the account) without any countermand of his former orders; he therefore prays the House to make such provision for his materials and labour in the premises as to them shall seem meet. Ordered to lie on the table."[1]

With this coffin-maker's memorial, so far as I have been able to trace it, ends the authentic history of the French Neutrals in Pennsylvania. All the rest is tradition; and with tradition, that fruitful source of error, I have nothing to do. Mr. Watson, in his Annals, tells us that for a long time the remnant of the Neutrals occupied a row of frame huts on the north side of Pine street, between Fifth and Sixth, on property owned either by Mr. Powel or Mr. Emlen; and those ruined houses, known as the Neutral Huts, are remembered distinctly by persons now living. What at last became of these poor creatures, it is not easy to ascertain from evidence. Their very names have perished. I have diligently searched the earliest extant Directories, and cannot find any one of the name that are known to us as belonging to them.

One other fact, proved by the official records, is that which I have already alluded to, that from November, 1755, till the Revolution, when ruder cares occupied the

[1] Votes, 465.

attention of our Pennsylvania legislators, there appears to have been expended for the support of the exiles, by public authority alone, aside from private benefaction — always bountiful in Philadelphia — no less a sum than £7500, currency, or about $20,000.

In this retrospect of a sad chapter of local history, I find nothing to wound the proper pride or excite the blush of Pennsylvania, and nowhere a trace of truth to justify the wanton aspersion on our fame, that Pennsylvania sold, or wished to sell, or thought of selling, these or any other human beings into slavery. The only colour for it comes in the shape of a very slight tradition embalmed in Mr. Vaux's Life of Benezet. It is this: "Such was Benezet's care of the Neutrals, that it produced a jealousy in the mind of one of the oldest men among them, of a very novel and curious description, which was communicated to a friend of Benezet, to whom he said: 'It is impossible that all this kindness can be disinterested; Mr. Benezet must certainly intend to recompense himself by treacherously selling us.' When their patron and protector," adds Mr. Vaux, "was informed of this ungrateful suspicion, it was so far from producing an emotion of anger or indignation, that he lifted up his hands and laughed immoderately."[1] Pointless as this gossiping anecdote is, the aspersion on our character rests on no other foundation. I have tracked the humble story of the Acadian exiles through authentic and official proofs, with little or no aid from contemporary correspondence, though much may exist that I have not had access to. There is no allusion to the Neutrals in the Shippen Papers, or in that far more inte-

[1] Life of Benezet, 88.

resting and valuable collection, the Hamilton MSS.; and Dr. Franklin, who wrote letters and pamphlets on almost every subject, and who was in Philadelphia when the Neutrals came, and for months afterwards, is silent about them. I have no doubt, however, that my vindication rests upon truth.

And closing this little essay, written rapidly, and at such short intervals as I have been able to snatch from daily drudgery, I cannot but recall the moral with which I began, made more pointed by the reflection the sad history suggests, that no kindness, no charity, no compassion can heal entirely the wound which religious persecution inflicts on the heart of man; no sympathy, slow or active, can lull to rest resentments which a sense of such wrong excites. These poor Catholic fugitives died in their faith. They hugged it to their wasted bosoms more closely, because they were persecuted and exiles. They died heartbroken, and the stain of their agony rests on the English name. It is made immortal, as I have said, in poetry of the English language; for Evangeline will live long after the feeble, persecuting statesmen of George the Second's reign are forgotten. Let those — and there seems a sort of centenary cycle in matters of this kind — who would persecute or proscribe for opinion's sake, and limit by political exclusion the right to worship God in the form which he who worships chooses; who would, if let alone, join in the hunt or exile of those who, like the Acadians, cherish the faith of their childhood and their ancestors, let them read this story, and beware of the sure retribution of history.

Should the opportunity occur, and, what is far more uncertain, the inclination continue, I hope on some future day to read a paper, as desultory as this, on the next visit of the French to Philadelphia; when, twenty-five years later, they came here triumphant, our welcome auxiliaries; when French noblemen and French priests were about the streets; and when, perhaps, as we may hope, they walked across the Potters' Field, which I remember, to Pine and Sixth streets, to look at the mouldering remains of the Neutral huts, or trace out the Neutral graves.

A RELATION OF THE MISFORTUNES OF THE FRENCH NEUTRALS,

As laid before the Assembly of the Province of Pennsylvania.

BY JOHN BAPTISTE GALERM,
ONE OF THE SAID PEOPLE.[1]

ABOUT the year 1713, when *Annapolis Royal* was taken from the *French*, our Fathers being then settled on the Bay of *Fundi*, upon the Surrender of that Country to the *English*, had, by virtue of the Treaty of Utrecht, a Year granted them to remove with their Effects; but not being willing to lose the Fruit of many Years labour, they chose rather to remain there, and become Subjects of *Great Britain*, on Condition that they might be exempted from bearing Arms against *France* (most of them having near Relations and Friends amongst the *French*, which they might have destroyed with their own Hands, had they consented to bear Arms against them). This Request they always understood to be granted, on their taking the Oath of Fidelity to her late Majesty, Queen *Anne;* which Oath of Fidelity was by us, about 27 Years ago, renewed to his Majesty, King *George*, by General *Philipse*, who then allowed us an Exemption of bearing Arms against *France;* which Exemption, till lately, (that we were told to the contrary) we always thought was approved of by the King. Our Oath of Fidelity, we that are now brought into this Province, as well as those of our Community that are carried into the neighbouring Provinces, have always inviolably observed, and have, on all Occasions, been willing to afford all the Assistance in our Power to his Majesty's Governors in erecting Forts, making Roads, Bridges, &c., and providing Provisions for his Majesty's Service, as can be testified by the several Governors and Officers that have commanded in his Majesty's Province of *Nova Scotia;* and this, notwithstanding the repeated Sollicitations, Threats, and Abuses, which we have continually, more or less, suffered from the *French* and *French Indians* of *Canada* on that Account, particularly about ten Years ago, when 500 *French* and *Indians* came to our Settlements, intending to attack *Annapolis Royal*, which, had their Intention succeeded, would have

[1] Broadside, in a Volume of the Pennsylvania Gazette, Philadelphia Library, Folio No. 992. As it follows the paper issue, No. 1418, of February 26, 1756, I presume that is about the date of its publication. It is proper to state that, from the absence of Mr. Reed in China, as Minister Plenipotentiary from the United States, the foregoing paper has not received his correction, in passing through the ress.—T. WARD.

made them Masters of all *Nova Scotia*, it being the only Place of Strength then in that Province, they earnestly sollicited us to join with, and aid them therein; but we persisting in our Resolution to abide true to our Oath of Fidelity, and absolutely refusing to give them any Assistance, they gave over their Intention, and returned to *Canada*. And about seven Years past, at the settling of *Halifax*, a Body of 150 *Indians* came amongst us, forced some of us from our Habitations, and by Threats and Blows would have compelled us to assist them in Way-laying and destroying the *English*, then employed in erecting Forts in different Parts of the Country; but we positively refusing, they left us, after having abused us, and made great Havock of our Cattle, &c. I myself was six Weeks before I wholly recovered of the Blows I received from them at that Time. Almost numberless are the Instances which might be given of the Abuses and Losses we have undergone from the *French Indians*, on Account of our steady Adherance to our Oath of Fidelity; and yet, notwithstanding our strict Observance thereof, we have not been able to prevent the grievous Calamity which is now come upon us, which we apprehend to be in a great Measure owing to the unhappy Situation and Conduct of some of our People settled at *Chiegnecto*, at the Bottom of the Bay of *Fundi*, where the *French*, about four Years ago, erected a Fort; those of our People who were settled near it, after having had many of their Settlements burnt by the *French*, being too far from *Halifax* and *Annapolis Royal* to expect sufficient Assistance from the *English*, were obliged, as we believe, more through Compulsion and Fear than Inclination, to join with and assist the *French*; which also appears from the Articles of Capitulation agreed on between Colonel *Monckton* and the *French* Commander, at the Delivery of the said Fort to the *English*, which is exactly in the following words.

[1] *With regard to the* Acadians, *as they have been forced to take up Arms on Pain of Death, they shall be pardoned for the Part they have been taking.* Notwithstanding this, as these People's Conduct had given just Umbrage to the Government, and created suspicions to the Prejudice of our whole Community, we were summoned to appear before the Governor and Council at *Halifax*, where we were required to take the Oath of Allegiance, without any exception, which we could not comply with, because, as that Government is at present situate, we apprehend we should have been obliged to take up Arms; but were still willing to take Oath of Fidelity, and give the strongest Assurances of continuing peaceable and faithful to his *Britannick* Majesty, with that Exception. But this, in the present Situation of Affairs, not being Satisfactory, we were made Prisoners, and our Estates, both real and personal, forfeited for the King's Use; and

[1] Gentleman's Magazine for July, 1755, Page 332.

Vessels being provided, we were sometime after sent off, with most of our Families, and dispersed among the *English* Colonies. The Hurry and Confusion in which we were embarked was an aggravating Circumstance attending our Misfortunes; for thereby many, who had lived in Affluence, found themselves deprived of every Necessary, and many Families were separated, Parents from Children, and Children from Parents. Yet blessed be God that it was our Lot to be sent to *Pennsylvania*, where our Wants have been relieved, and we have in every Respect been received with Christian Benevolence and Charity. And let me add, that notwithstanding the Suspicions and Fears which many here are possessed of on our Account, as tho' we were a dangerous People, who make little Scruple of breaking our Oaths, Time will manifest that we are not such a People: No, the unhappy Situation which we are now in, is a plain Evidence that this is a false Charge, tending to aggravate the Misfortunes of an already too unhappy People; for, had we entertained such pernicious Sentiments, we might easily have prevented our falling into the melancholy Circumstances we are now in, *viz:* Deprived of our Substance, banished from our native Country, and reduced to live by Charity in a strange Land; and this for refusing to take an Oath, which we are firmly persuaded Christianity absolutely forbids us to violate, had we once taken it, and yet an Oath which we could not comply with, without being exposed to plunge our Swords in the Breasts of our Friends and Relations. We shall, however, as we have hitherto done, submit to what, in the present Situation of Affairs, may seem necessary, and with Patience and Resignation bear whatever God, in the Course of his Providence, shall suffer to come upon us. We shall also think it our Duty to seek and promote the Peace of the Country into which we are transported, and inviolably keep the Oath of Fidelity that we have taken to his gracious Majesty, King *George*, whom we firmly believe, when fully acquainted with our Faithfulness and Sufferings, will commiserate our unhappy Condition, and order that some Compensation be made us for our Losses. And may the Almighty abundantly bless his Honour, the Governor, the honourable Assembly of the Province, and the good People of *Philadelphia*, whose Sympathy, Benevolence, and Christian Charity, have been, and still are, greatly manifested and extended towards us, a poor distressed and afflicted People, is the Sincere and earnest Prayer of

JOHN BAPTISTE GALERM.

www.ingramcontent.com/pod-product-compliance
Lightning Source LLC
LaVergne TN
LVHW011133110826
845150LV00008B/2327

* 9 7 8 1 4 1 8 1 9 4 4 5 1 *